THE VOLUNTEER CODE

HOW TO RECRUIT AND CARE FOR VOLUNTEERS

RYAN FRANK

The Volunteer Code: How to Recruit and Care for Volunteers
by Ryan Frank

copyright ©2016 Ryan Frank

Trade paperback ISBN: 978-1-943294-41-1
Ebook ISBN: 978-1-943294-42-8

Cover design by Martijn van Tilborgh

Pulse is also available on Amazon Kindle, Barnes & Noble
Nook and Apple iBooks.

Published by Leverage Group

CONTENTS

FOREWORD

IF YOU ARE READING THIS Foreword, chances are you purchased this book for one or both of these two reasons: 1) All of us in ministry need fresh ideas on how to recruit and care for workers. 2) You know if Ryan Frank's put out a new book, it's going to be full of practical, useful information that comes from his heart and from experience.

I first met Ryan over a decade ago. I had heard of this young and up-and-coming leader and wanted to meet him. I was impressed by his zeal and drive as well as his unique ability and desire to not just think and do what everyone else was thinking and doing. Ryan was one of those rare leaders who dared to dream and think big. He was not afraid to walk out his dreams and try and do new things to get different results. From that point to this, Ryan and I have joined forces on multiple projects not just because I like him and respect him (which are both true statements), but because every time I'm around him and work with him, I learn something. Out of these experiences have birthed a deep friendship that I am thankful for. I know I can call Ryan day or night, and he will pray with me or for me and give me wise counsel and input.

I have had the privilege of working at churches of every size from small to huge. At every church, no matter the size, I have learned you will never stop recruiting and caring for workers.

I believe the tasks and ministry functions like recruiting and caring for others and building a great ministry team will only happen when we realize that these things are worth our time, effort and energy to develop. This book will help you develop these skills. So many times we read books that give us good ideas and the why behind a subject. Ryan's books go a step beyond and give you how. You'll get action steps to put this information into practical, easy-to-follow steps that you can do. These steps have been proven in a local church, and they actually work.

Recruiting is not a game of "Red Rover" where you learn the magic words and can simply say "Red Rover, Red Rover, send workers right over." There is no magic pill in recruiting, so get that out of your head. That's not what this book is all about. You'll find the whys, but you'll also find the what, when, where and hows. This book will help you change your thinking about your own abilities and help move you from "I can't" to "I can."

Years ago the Lord ask me a question that changed me forever. (If you've read any of my books or heard me teach on recruiting, you've probably heard me say this.) I was praying that the Lord would send laborers, like He asked us to do, when I heard in my spirit say, "Why should I give you any more workers if you are not caring for the ones you already have?" That question not only rocked my world then -- it rocks my world today. All of us in ministry have been given a job in 1 Peter 5:2 – "Be shepherds of God's flock that is under your care, watching over them—not because you must, but because you are willing, as God wants you to be..." I believe this responsibility to feed, care and give oversight is not just for the children and students we lead, but also for those workers God has placed in our care so that we can help grow them and care for them to be the disciples, the leaders, the Moms and Dads, and the husbands and wives they need to be. You'll learn how to better care for the workers God has given you from the heart of a Pastor. So what are you waiting for? Quit reading my ramblings about my good friend's new book and dig in with an open mind and heart to walk out and do what this book says. I believe that if you will, you'll experience personal growth as well as growth in your ministry.

Jim Wideman
Children's and Family Ministry Pioneer
www.jimwideman.com

DEDICATION

For Jesus, who taught me how to recruit and care for volunteers.

INTRODUCTION

THANKS FOR TAKING TIME TO read this book. I am both humbled and eager for you to dig in and have a volunteer breakthrough like never before.

I've been a pastor for nearly 20 years. I lead a nonprofit. I have served on boards of nonprofits. I have coached and mentored a lot of ministry and nonprofit leaders. Over the course of my life, I've learned that churches and nonprofits really live or die based upon their volunteers. For a lot of churches and nonprofits, volunteers are their very staff. It's the people you rely on the very most. And without those volunteers, you would be in a world of hurt.

We have a great teacher. Not me. It's the Lord, Jesus Christ. Jesus spent 33 years of His life teaching us how to relate to people. He taught us how to understand people and, really, how to move people from being volunteers to ministers. Think about His 12 disciples. Those guys started as people who volunteered to follow Him, and they moved quickly. Some of them moved quicker than others. They learned to move from being a volunteer to becoming an invested leader. All in favor of having invested leaders, raise your hand right now where you are. That's what you want isn't it?

In this course, I'm going to share with you my ten laws for having a volunteer breakthrough. I didn't come up with all this. Like I said, Jesus is the greatest teacher. I mean, Jesus got all of this. And there have been a lot of leaders in history who have understood this. So one thing I enjoy doing is finding leaders who have had volunteer breakthroughs and learning from them, gleaning as much information as I can. So in my time of learning and studying great leaders, things I've experienced in my own life and my own ministry in leadership, I have identified ten laws that I believe you need to put into practice if you're going to have a volunteer breakthrough.

Hey, I get it. It's a challenge. Working with volunteers is a challenge. Getting volunteers is a challenge, keeping volunteers is a challenge, moving people from a volunteer mentality to an invested leader mentality – that's a challenge. I understand that, but I also understand this: it brings the greatest reward.

By practicing these ten laws, and by understanding them and making them a part of your day-to-day leadership in your organization, I believe that you can have a volunteer breakthrough like never before.

Let's dig in.

Law No. 1 is human need. Everyone has basic needs like love, appreciation, and community.

Law No. 2 is the law of recruiting. Flyers don't recruit people and advertisements don't recruit people. You may get a few, but the truth is that people recruit people.

Law No. 3 is the law of vision. You have to have a strong, big vision and be able to convey it to others so that they buy into you and the vision.

Law No. 4 is the law of the plan. What's your plan? What positions do you need? Not only now, but what's your plan for growth? If you're going to grow, what do you need?

Law No. 5 is the law of the ask. You can have a great vision. You can have a great plan and you can understand human needs, but if you never ask people to help you, you're not going to get very far. This comes easy for some and is very difficult for others.

Law No. 6 is the law of best fit. You have figure out where volunteers best fit. How has God wired them – their gifts, talents, and abilities? What are the unique needs of your ministry and where's the best meeting of the two?

Law No. 7 is the law of training. We'll get practical and address how you train people in today's economy – not just the financial economy, but the time economy. People are so busy and time is a precious commodity.

Law No. 8 is the law of excellence. Excellent ministries attract excellent people. Excellent leaders attract excellent people. I believe that, because you are a part of this course, you want to achieve excellence.

Law No. 9 is the law of appreciation. It's been said that if you want more volunteers, make heroes of the ones you already have. You have to learn how to appreciate volunteers.

Law No. 10 is the law of the shepherd. Your volunteers don't get paid. They're not on your benefits package. So if you're going to continue to lead them and keep them engaged, you have to learn how to shepherd and care for them.

In each chapter, I'll break down that law to help you understand the significance each plays in having a volunteer breakthrough in your organization. Then I'll go beyond the teaching and help you think through what the law can look like for you in your ministry or organization.

Every person has a unique DNA, right? And every organization has a unique DNA. So how does this apply to you and your church or organization? At the end of each chapter is the Game Plan – a place for you to write down your takeaways. You need a personal strategy in place to keep you accountable and as something for you to review on a regular basis.

Are you ready to experience a volunteer breakthrough?

THE LAW OF HUMAN NEED

HUMAN NEED HASN'T CHANGED MUCH since Adam and Eve. There have been a lot of people on earth since Adam and Eve, but human needs haven't changed a whole lot. The same stuff that Adam and Eve, Moses and Abraham, and David and Queen Esther dealt with in the Old Testament and the stuff that Mary and Joseph and the Apostle Paul and Cornelius dealt with in the New Testament is what we deal with today. Human need hasn't changed a lot but how you approach it has. If you understand human need, it could very well be the key that unlocks your volunteer breakthrough. There are some basic needs that every human has, and when you understand these needs, you can bring them in alignment with what you need in your ministry.

PEOPLE NEED TO BE LOVED

First of all, everyone has a need to be loved. This is something God placed within you. Do you remember the movie *Toy Story*? I love *Toy Story 1, 2,* and *3*. In *Toy Story 1*, if you remember, Buzz and Woody are trapped in Sid's house, the mean kid from next door. While they're in Sid's house, Buzz finally realizes that he is not unique; he is one of hundreds of thousands of toys. Here he's thought thinks he was the only one and that he was a real astronaut. Sheriff Woody has been trying to tell him that he's just a toy. When he realizes he's just a toy, he's ready to give it all up. Then Woody says something along these lines: There is nothing more important in the world than being loved by a kid.

Many of you are in children's ministry. You work with kids and/or families. There is nothing more significant than being loved by a child, and every person has the need to be loved. Question: how well do you love your people?

Corrie ten Boom is one of my heroes of the faith. She said this: "If the devil cannot make us bad, he will make us busy." Truthfully, some of us are so busy that we don't have time to love people the way we should. How well are you loving people? Your prayer each day should be: "God, give me a greater capacity to love people. People need to be loved."

PEOPLE NEED TO BE NEEDED

One of your greatest needs in your ministry or organization is recruiting people, right? If you're a nonprofit or church leader, you need volunteers. I'm going to tell you this right now. There are people out there who would love to work with you, but they need to be asked.

I understand, especially when working with Christians that Christians ought to volunteer to serve. I get that. But there are people who are shy and timid. There are people who don't know you, so they're not going to be comfortable coming up to you and talking with you. Or there are people who just assume that the ministry is well staffed. They don't know what the needs are. There are people out there who, if you ask them to serve, will say yes. I guarantee it. They just need to know that you need them.

PEOPLE NEED COMMUNITY

This is why a billion people are on Facebook. Although Facebook is a real part of our world and it can be influential in how we move people from volunteers to invested leaders, having a real spirit of community is very difficult in this digital world. Why? Because people live on their phones, they live on the internet, and they live in front of a computer and TV screen.

If you foster community with your volunteers in your church or organization, you're not going to have a volunteer shortage problem because it's their small group. Those volunteers aren't going to quit. You're not going to be able to shake them off with a stick because this is their community – the place where they belong and find purpose.

PEOPLE NEED TO BE UNDERSTOOD

Jesus was a master at this. Jesus understood people. Do you remember the woman who was caught in the act of adultery? Think about what was going on in her heart. She was dragged out in front of all of the leaders of the city. Just think of the humiliation, the terror that was going on in her heart. There she stood, accused. And the city leaders were picking up stones because the law said she was to be stoned. Then Jesus knelt down and wrote in the sand.

Now, it bothers me that the scripture doesn't say what He wrote in the sand. That's going to be one of my first questions when I get to heaven. But whatever He wrote was significant because they all left. Then Jesus looked up and asked the woman where her accusers were and if even one of them condemned her. She said no and then Jesus said, "Neither do I. Go and sin no more" (John 8:11b ESV).

Jesus understood the needs of that woman. He understood what was going on in her heart. He was the Son of God and He came to set an example of what it means to understand others. How can you understand people? Let me give you a few ideas.

BE FRIENDLY

Smile. Some people have a hard time smiling. Early in my ministry I was so busy at the church, I would run, run, run,

run, run. I'd often have people ask me, "Hey, are you mad? Why do you always look like you're mad?" I wasn't mad, but I was so serious and focused that I would run without talking to people, without even saying hi to people. I've learned over the years that if I'm going to connect with people, I have to be friendly. So I began to force myself to smile whenever I was around people, and now it's become a habit. Maybe some of you need to remind yourself to be friendly.

LEARN THE ART OF SMALL TALK

Converse with your volunteers. Not about work, not about the church, not about the ministry, not about the day that's ahead of you, but just small talk. Lighten up a little bit. Be friendly. Understand people.

BE VULNERABLE

For you to understand people, you have to be willing to allow people to understand you. So there's some vulnerability that has to take place. Of course you have to be careful whom you're vulnerable with. And there is a time and place for various topics of conversation and there are certain topics you should not discuss openly, such as private things the church staff is working through or who they are helping. But you can and should be vulnerable – be known so other will allow you to know them.

As you understand people, they will understand you. They will begin to understand your heart for the ministry, and they will move from being just a volunteer to becoming an invested leader. They will become people who have bought into you, your ministry, your vision, and your strategy.

PEOPLE NEED ENCOURAGEMENT

Think about the average day of a volunteer or any human being and how many negative things happen in that person's life. Think about how one word of encouragement can take away all of that negativity. Encouragement is so powerful.

There are lots of ways to encourage people. Write thank you notes. Do you remember thank you notes? I mean, this is back before email and texting and before you sent someone a thank you via Facebook. Do you remember when you sat down to write a thank you note? For the last 15 years, not a week has gone by that I don't write at least three to five thank you notes to people who come to my mind.

For example: "Hey, Becky. Thank you. I saw you on the floor reading a story to those two-year-olds on Sunday. I just want you to know that we are blessed to have you in our church. Thank you so much for investing in our kids."

What does that take you? It takes you about 45 seconds and the cost of a stamp.

This morning on my way to the office I thought of someone. And you know what I thought? That person is a blessing to me. You know what I did? As soon as I got to the office I sent that person a text and said, "I want you to know that the Lord brought you to my mind this morning. Thank you for being my friend."

I could have just thought that and never expressed anything to that person, but I did not want to rob that person of a blessing. People need to be encouraged. Encouragement goes a long way.

PEOPLE NEED TO FEEL IMPORTANT

People need to feel like they're part of something important. Do you let your volunteers know that they're doing something important, that they're part of the most important ministry or organization in your city? They need to know that what they're doing is highly valued.

There are lot of ways you can make volunteers feel important. Again, you can send thank you notes. Give appreciation gifts every so often. Pass out a $5.00 Starbucks or Dunkin' Donuts gift card. Take your volunteers out to lunch.

You can do appreciation events. I was invited a few years back to speak at an appreciation event. I had met a children's pastor at a conference, and she invited me to her church just about an hour or two from my home. She said dress as formal as you can. The theme was a night with the stars. When I pulled up, they had the red carpet out – literally. They had the kids in the youth group valet parking our cars. And they had the other youth out with cameras like the paparazzi. They had hors d'oeuvres and they served the dinner on china. It was a night with the stars. They were saying, "We believe that what you're doing is so very important."

There are people in your church or your organization who won't get in front of a group of people to teach, but they will pray. Find people who will be your ministry's prayer partners. Ask these people to pray for specific volunteers. How amazing will it be when you can go to every one of your volunteers and say, "You know what? This person in the church is your prayer partner and will be praying for you every week."

What kind of an impact would this have on your volunteers if they knew someone was praying for them by name each week? I guarantee you there would be some good results there. Those volunteer won't be quick to quit.

PEOPLE NEED SIGNIFICANCE

This is one reason why you need to be very, very careful about rotating volunteers. When you rotate volunteers once a month or every other month, they can develop the mentality that they're just filling a slot. Sometimes you have to rotate workers, and I understand that. If you do need to rotate volunteers, you have to work extra hard to make sure they realize that even though they are rotated in various places and times, they are essential.

When I recruit teachers, I don't ask them to teach on a rotation. I ask them to teach for life. When I study the scripture, I find that a calling to teach is a calling for life. We will get more into this when we get to Law No. 5, which is the law of the ask. I ask people to teach either until their gifts change, their calling changes, or until they die. And if they ever need a break, I give them a break, but I ask them to teach because I believe what we're doing is very significant. And I understand one of the basic human needs that God has wired us with is a need to do things with significance. People want to leave a legacy. They want to be a part of something significant.

PEOPLE NEED CERTAINTY

You need job and financial security. You need a place to call home every night. People have this basic human need for security and certainty in their life. Because of this basic need, you need to have a well-planned, well-structured ministry or organization. One that causes people to think, *Wow, these people leading this thing, they know what they're doing. They have a plan.* More about that when we get to Law No. 4, the law of the plan.

Do your volunteers know what the expectations are of them? Do they know that what they do fits into the big picture? How well are you doing with communication? Do you have a clear, set plan and program in place that provides the certainty and security that people need?

PEOPLE NEED PRAYER

Do you pray for your volunteers and for people who aren't your volunteers? If you're a ministry leader, you know what it's like before or after church. You're busy. And how many times has someone come up to you and said, "Hey, would you pray about this?" Or the phone rings before church. I hate it when my phone rings before church because I know that means that someone can't be in their volunteer role that morning. So when that volunteer calls me and says, "Hey, I'm not going to be there today because so and so is sick or something happened at work."

Instead of telling the person that I'll pray about it, I ask if we can pray right there. Why? Because you're not going to pray about it; you're going to forget about it. Why not just stop and pray right then? These are what I call 30-second foyer prayers. It doesn't mean you have to pray for ten minutes. It can be a 20- to 30-second prayer. Because this is a need that people have and stopping everything for 30 seconds will mean more than you know.

FINAL THOUGHT

As you think about the basic human needs of people, I want you to think about how you are doing right now.

Think about these nine basic human needs: Everybody needs to be loved, needed, to be in community, to be understood, they need to be encouraged, to feel like they're a part of something important, they need significance, they need certainty, and to be prayed for. How well are you doing in these areas?

On the next page is your Game Plan. I want you to create some action steps on the next few pages, and I want you to identify three of these areas that you need to grow in. I don't want your action steps to be all ten. You will never do them all. I want you to find three and focus on them.

Then I want you to do this. After you've identified the top three, specify a few things that you're going to begin doing right away to address them.

MY GAME PLAN

THE LAW OF RECRUITING

THERE COMES A POINT WHERE you have to ask people to help you. You have to ask people to work for you, to volunteer their time for you. I don't know if you have learned it yet, but let me say that, from my experience and the hundreds of ministry leaders and nonprofit leaders that I've worked with, advertisements do not recruit people. Flyers do not recruit people. Doing a little blurb in the church bulletin does not recruit people. Memorandums do not recruit people. Putting something on a website does not recruit people.

The secret is that people recruit people. If you study those who are successful in recruiting, you will find that they do not rely on advertisements or flyers. They do not rely on classified ads. They recruit people. Or if they don't recruit people, they get other people to recruit people. This is the way it works.

One of my great friends is Roger Fields. He leads a ministry called Kidz Blitz, which does family and children's ministry large, mega stage events in churches and in other areas. I got an email from him some time ago where he communicated the concept that begging people to volunteer doesn't work. In fact, he goes as far as saying that begging will kill your ministry.

He uses a great example. Do you remember the Sermon on the Mount? Imagine if Jesus were preaching the Sermon on the Mount, and if he would have said, "Hey, you know what? I am a couple of disciples short. If you want to help me, if you want to follow me, there is a guy named Peter over there standing by that tree, and he has a clipboard. Just go sign up on the clipboard, and someone will reach out to you in the next 7 to 14 days, and we'll let you know what's involved."

But Jesus didn't do it that way because it would have cheapened the calling of a disciple. Jesus didn't cheapen the calling. He was specific. He personally asked people to be His disciple. Begging will kill your ministry. Begging and cattle calls communicates that you're desperate and will settle for anybody.

SECRET #1:
PEOPLE RECRUIT PEOPLE

You might think you don't have the time to recruit the way it really needs to be done. You may legitimately have so much going on, that you truly don't have the time. Then you need to get other people to recruit for you.

SECRET #2:
BEFORE YOU CAN SELL YOUR MINISTRY, YOU HAVE TO SELL YOURSELF

If you want to recruit more people and you want invested leaders, people who are going to buy into the vision and mission, they first have to buy into you. This is why you need to energize your people skills.

I don't care what size budget you have. I don't care what size program you have. If you fail in this area of people skills, your ministry and programs are going to fail. In fact, I've found in my work and experience that the majority of people who fail in ministry do so because they lack people skills. they haven't failed for lack of education or technical expertise. They fail because they don't know how to treat and work with people.

It's been said that if you want your ministry to shine, you have to polish your people skills. And I would add this: If you want to recruit more volunteers, if you want to keep more volunteers for the long haul, and you want to move people from being a volunteer to being an invested leader, you have to improve your people skills. People have to buy into you. So let me give you some tips on how to do this.

BE THE SERVANT YOU WANT OTHERS TO BE

Jesus was a servant. What did he say in Philippians 2:5? He said, "Have this mind among yourselves, which is yours in Christ Jesus." He also said that, "the Son of Man came not to be served but to serve, and to give his life as a ransom for many" (Mark 10:45). Yes, He was God, but He came to set an example for us.

So much of ministry and so much of leadership is about being a servant. Jesus washed dirty feet to model this very principle. A lot of ministry, a lot of working with volunteers, is about foot washing.

When you purpose to be a servant to your volunteers and to others, your people skills are going to shine. You're going to find yourself three steps ahead of most people who are serving in the same capacity you are serving in. When you position yourself as a servant leader who wants to serve other people, people will line up to volunteer.

DON'T COMPLAIN

If you're going to grow your people skills, don't complain. We can all find things to complain about. How many times do you drive home from church on Sunday with your list? Boy, if just this would change or if the kids would do this or if my boss would do that.

Choose to be a person doesn't complain. Nobody wants to be around a Debbie downer. Volunteers want to be around encouraging people; people who don't complain and are uplifting in their conversations. I love to be around people like this, and people will love to be around you if you choose to not complain.

SMILE

This will take you far in improving your interpersonal skills. It doesn't matter how much knowledge you have or how good you are at your technical expertise. If you don't smile, what does your countenance communicate? Does your countenance communicate that you are a warm, pleasant person, who is approachable, or does your countenance communicate for people to bug off or you're too busy? If you want more volunteers, you need to make sure that you have a countenance that is approachable. Having an approachable countenance begins with a smile.

If you have a hard time smiling by nature, force it. It can become a habit. I know that might sound funny, but smiling can become a habit. Remember back to last chapter when I said I used to walk around my church not smiling because I was so focused and busy? I had to be intentional and force myself to smile until it became a habit.

BE A GOOD LISTENER

As leaders, we like to talk, and we have plenty to say, but how well do we listen? Remember when your mom or your grandma used to tell you that God gave you two ears and one mouth, so you can listen twice as much as you talk? If you want to grow your people skills, you need to learn to listen.

People can tell whether you're really listening or not. If you're not looking them in the eyes or you're looking around or checking your phone, you're not being a good listener.

Listening shows that you're interested and invested. And be sure to seek out to listen and be invested regardless of whether the person will be a volunteer.

MAKE PEOPLE FEEL IMPORTANT

You need to communicate to people that you can't do what you do without your volunteers or that the ministry would be in a world of hurt if it wasn't for them.

Whenever I'm around people, I want to be wind in their sails. When people leave my presence, I want them to feel important. When you start putting these skills into practice, you won't have a problem recruiting and keeping volunteers.

REMEMBER PEOPLE'S NAMES

If you're going to grow your people skills, remember people's names. Dale Carnegie, author of *How to Win Friends and Influence People,* said this: "The sweetest sound to anyone's ear—no matter what language it's in—is their own name."

Let me tell you how I've approached it over the years. I approach it just like I do scripture memory. When I memorize verses, I say that verse over and over and over again.

So if I meet you for the first time, here's how the conversation might go: "Hey, Luigi, it's great to meet you tonight. Man, thanks for coming. Luigi, have you ever been to the church before? No? Well, hey, where do you work, Luigi? That's awesome. I drive by there every day, Luigi. Hey, Luigi, how many kids do you have? Okay, great. I have three, Luigi." By the time I've ended that 90- to 120-second conversation, I have said Luigi's name about 15 times, and it's going to stick with me.

If you're not intentional about memorizing people's names, what's going to happen? "Hey, Luigi, it's great to meet you. Hope to see you next week." After you turn and walk away, you have already forgotten that person's name.

We are we spending a lot of time to talk about developing people skills. Because Law No. 2 is the law of recruiting, and people recruit people. If you're going to be an excellent recruiter of people, you have to polish your people skills. Make it a daily habit.

FINAL THOUGHT

First, how are your people skills? Be honest. Here's a way to identify how you're doing on your people skills. Ask some other people. Ask a co-worker or your spouse. We can all grow in this area. Then based upon what you discover determine what areas you need to grow in to have better people skills.

Second, what are you currently doing to recruit people? Are you relying on advertisements? Are you relying on classified ads? Are you relying on newsletters? Are you relying on announcements from the pulpit? Those aren't effective. People recruit people.

Third, what should you do differently starting right now?

Think through these questions and answer them in your Game Plan. Then get busy!

MY GAME PLAN

_____
_____
_____
_____
_____
_____
_____
_____
_____
_____
_____
_____
_____
_____
_____
_____
_____
_____
_____
_____
_____
_____
_____
_____
_____

_____

_____

_____

_____

_____

_____

_____

_____

_____

_____

_____

_____

_____

_____

_____

_____

_____

_____

_____

_____

_____

_____

_____

_____

_____

_____

_____

THE LAW OF VISION

VISION IS PROBABLY THE MOST powerful thing you can possess as a leader. As leaders, when we talk about vision, we're talking about seeing what other people don't see. Your vision is what you are working toward. Your vision is what you are moving after, and ultimately what you want is a team to come alongside you and move toward that vision as well.

Great leaders in history were persuaded by a vision. It goes back to the Bible. One person who comes to mind is Nehemiah. Nehemiah wanted to rebuild the walls, so he persuaded the king to let him go. The king even sent money and his blessing. While the people were rebuilding the wall, the enemy attacked them. And so Nehemiah had tools in one hand and a sword in the other, fighting off the enemies. His vision drove him forward, and the vision drove other people around him who were all about getting those walls finished.

Modern history is full of visionaries. Nelson Mandela wanted to see South Africa without racial integration. Susan B. Anthony wanted women to have the right to vote. President John F. Kennedy had a great vision for the space program. He said we were going to the moon.

What kind of vision do you have for your organization or ministry? What is it that you see that other people don't see? What vision do you want others to see? How will you share that vision and gather others around you who will share it too? People want to follow a leader with vision. You probably get that. I would say there's a good chance that whatever job you have today, you are in that position because of a leader who has vision and you were compelled to join that organization and to follow that leader in the vision that God has given him or her.

The *Harvard Business Review* did a research project a few years back where they studied lots of people in the workforce and asked them this question: What is it that draws you, what do you look for, what do you admire in a leader? The top answer was honesty. People look for honesty in leaders. Are you an honest leader? Are you a man or a woman of integrity? Is who you portray yourself to be during the day the same person as you are at night? When you're by yourself, are you the same person who people think you are? People will follow a leader they can trust.

The second answer is that people want a leader who is forward thinking. They want a leader who is a visionary, who can see down the road, who can see things that they don't see but that they can rally behind. So with that being said, I want to help you think through a vision for your ministry, for your nonprofit, for your organization, or whatever your context.

There are five things you need to do if you are going to determine a vision and get people to rally behind it.

GET ALONE

First, you have to get alone. If you're going to be able to determine a vision for your organization, you're not going to get that vision unless you step away from the day-to-day busyness and schedule. You may eventually choose to get alone with your spouse or you may choose to get alone with your core team, but where it starts is being completely alone.

You might have to schedule time away. I have three little girls at home, so I don't have the luxury of renting a cabin in the woods by myself for a week. I want to be with my wife and girls. But I will schedule days where I don't go into the office. I lock myself in a room at home or take a day trip to a location where I can be by myself.

Especially if you're a Christian leader and if you lead a Christian organization or church, this is important. Because you don't just want your vision; you want God's vision. This is where you begin to pick up steam, when God has an idea and when you have an idea, and these two ideas come together, that's where the momentum begins to pick up and where exciting things begin to happen.

Jim Wideman told me once, "I don't have a vision – a vision has me!" I didn't create some vision. I caught a vision. That vision comes from getting alone and spending time with God.

OBSERVE YOUR CURRENT WORLD

You not only need to get alone with God, but you need to take an honest observation of your world (your current organization or ministry). Evaluate where you are and do a SWOT analysis.

SWOT stands for strengths, weaknesses, opportunities, and threats. What are the current strengths of your organization? What are the current weaknesses or vulnerable spots? What are the opportunities that exist for your organization? What are the open doors? What could you be doing? And finally, what are the threats? What has the potential to dismantle your organization?

I like to pull our senior team at KidzMatter aside once a year and do an honest SWOT analysis. We check our pride at the door and get really honest because this type of in-depth analysis is what will lead to growth and maturity.

WRITE DOWN WHAT YOU WOULD LIKE TO SEE IN THE FUTURE

As you look to the future, what would you like to see? This is a key right here - write it down. This is one reason why you have a section at the end of each chapter called My Game Plan. You need to write things down. Something magical happens when you write your thoughts down on paper.

As you study your world and analyze it, you also need to analyze other organizations and ministries. Research. Read. Interview. As you do these things you also pray that the Holy Spirit would show what He wants for your ministry. And as the Holy Spirit guides and directs, write it all down.

SHARE YOUR VISION

After you have a vision in place, meet with your team; those who support you and work for you. This probably isn't your entire team but it should be your core team. These key stakeholders are who you have to get to buy in or it's not going to work.

Here's something important to remember at this point: Your vision isn't concrete yet. Step No. 3 was YOU are beginning to write down what YOU believe the future is going to look like. But where this gets really powerful is when you share your vision with your key stakeholders, which means you allow them to speak into the vision and you are mature enough as a leader that you are willing to make some adaptations based upon what the key stakeholders have to say.

I can have a vision. In my mind, all the dots can be connected. But key stakeholders will say, "Now, just a minute. Do those dots really connect? Or maybe we should think about it from this angle."

So you share what God has given you with your key stakeholders, and together come up with a shared vision. Shared vision is huge. If you have a shared vision with your key stakeholders, you are going to be way ahead of others who are doing what you do. You can't force your vision on others and expect it to end well.

COMMUNICATE YOUR VISION DAILY

Once you have an established vision that you and your core team agree on, you need to communicate it often. It's your job as the leader to communicate the vision to your volunteers. Why don't they just get it like you got it? Because God didn't give them the vision. God gave it to you. And you've spent countless hours pondering and processing the vision. Your volunteers haven't.

So how do you communicate your vision? Creatively. Every organization and ministry is different. How your volunteers communicate is different. Gather every one together. Have lunch or dinner brought in, and dedicate time to conveying the vision, and they have been preceded by a vision meeting, the process of its inception, and how it will be carried out.

There are many ways to continue to share the vision. On the website, in monthly newsletters, in Facebook pages or groups. Done alone, these won't have much impact, but when all channels of information are conveying the same message and vision, they can have an impact. Put signs on the wall throughout the building, on bulletin boards, and on the doors. Any way you can communicate it, do it. And then you, as the leader, constantly communicate it too.

FINAL THOUGHT

When God gives you a vision for your ministry, when you can see what other people can't see, let me encourage you: Don't fret or don't panic over how are you're going to get there. Communicate the vision. Be an example of the vision and beg God for His blessing on the vision. Then watch as that vision begins to become a reality.

Now think about your Game Plan. Take some time to reflect. How are you doing with the law of vision? Do you have a vision for your ministry, for your organization? Is it vague? Is it old? Do volunteers even know what it is? What do you need to do and what is your first step? Put pen to paper and write it down.

MY GAME PLAN

_____

_____

_____

_____

_____

_____

_____

_____

_____

_____

_____

_____

_____

_____

_____

_____

_____

_____

_____

_____

_____

_____

_____

_____

THE LAW OF THE PLAN

A PLAN IS THE KEY TO ANY business. When working on a start-up business, if you want investors, you have to have a strong plan. People want to see the plan before they will invest. As a leader, a plan helps you know where to allocate your resources.

A plan will also keep you on mission. You don't want mission drift as an organizational leader. You want to stay true to your mission, and that's where a plan keeps you grounded and focused.

As you think through having a volunteer breakthrough, I want you to think about the plan you have in place as you recruit and engage volunteers. Here are some items to have in place in the law of the plan.

IDENTIFY THE POSITIONS

What are the positions that need to be filled within your organization? You would be amazed how many times I have someone come to me and say, "Oh, we can't get enough help. Our ministry is struggling for volunteers." Well, where do you need help? They say everywhere. Ok. Be more specific. They can't get specific. They know they need volunteers but they don't know what jobs need to be filled.

When you're engaging a new relationship with someone and you finally get to that point where he wants to help you, the worst thing that can happen is to tell him you'll get back with him, that you know you need help but don't know exactly where.

What you communicate to that person is the ministry isn't significant and organized. You need to know off the top of your head what positions you need to fill and be ready at the drop of a hat to name them.

By the way, the more you pray about open positions, the more they're going to be on your list, your radar, and on your brain. Pray that God will send the right people into your ministry or organization. When you do that, you will be more sensitive as you meet people and talk with them. You'll pick up on their skill sets and character traits and will know if they're a good fit and where to place them.

JOB DESCRIPTIONS: WHY AND HOW

It doesn't matter how small or large the task you have for a volunteer, every volunteer position deserves a job description. You may not call it a job description. You could call it a ministry description or service description. The name doesn't matter as much as having one for each role does. The job description should specify what is expected of the role.

Job descriptions are huge. Why? Let me give you a few reasons.

THEY PROVIDE THE QUALIFICATIONS

What are you looking for? Are you looking for someone over the age of 18? Are you looking for a married couple? Are you looking for someone with a college degree? Are we looking for someone who knows how to cook? Be specific in what skills are needed for the role.

THEY COMMUNICATE EXPECTATIONS

Don't leave anything to chance. Having a clear job description that specifies the expectations eliminates confusion. What is expected? Is it expected that she be prepared? Is it expected that he bring his own materials? Is it expected that she's going to buy materials and be reimbursed?

THEY SET BOUNDARIES

When you have a job description for a volunteer, it lets the person know the parameters. You might think, *Why would that person think he has the authority to make that decision?* Well, maybe it's because you never told him the boundaries. What gives her the right to think that she can spend that much money on that? Or what gives him the right to think that he can handle that? Well, again, the boundaries probably weren't established and made known to the volunteer. You can take care of that in a job description on the front end.

THEY COMMUNICATE SIGNIFICANCE

Remember Law No. 1, the law of human need? People want to be a part of something significant. When you have a job description for any volunteer position it communicates that this job is significant. This is something very important. If you took the time to put together the job description you convey that the job should be taken seriously.

THEY WILL SAVE YOU HEADACHES

It saves a headache not only for you, but also for your volunteers. If they know what the qualifications, expectations, boundaries, and the level of significance are beforehand, both you and they will be much more engaged and much less frustrated.

HOW TO WRITE A JOB DESCRIPTION

The following are some key elements for job descriptions.

START WITH A TITLE

Every volunteer position deserves a title. It doesn't matter if the job is cleaning the windows in the nursery or washing dishes or teaching High school youth. Every job needs a title.

IDENTIFY THE OBJECTIVE

The next part of a job description needs to be convey the objective: the reason this job is essential and important to the ministry or organization. Some examples are: This position is important because it furthers our mission, it assists families or children, aids in feeding people, etc. The objective should be a paragraph or less.

INCLUDE THE QUALIFICATIONS

List the things that are expected of a candidate. Some may be required while others are a plus. Specify which is which. Is there an age requirement? Does the volunteer need to provide his/her own transportation?

DISCLOSE THE RESPONSIBILITIES

What is the job? What will this volunteer do? List the key responsibilities. There might be 5 or 10. Play piano? Sit and chat with the elderly? Prep food? Make copies of coloring sheets? Provide as many of the responsibilities that you can think of so the volunteer doesn't get into the role and feel surprised or frustrated because he is being asked to do something he didn't know he needed to do.

GIVE THE TIME AND PLACE

You have to assume not everyone knows where and when. Use the LCD – the least common denominator. Think about the least common denominator out there, the person who's brand new and doesn't know where the elementary kids meet or where the kitchen is. This volunteer position serves every Tuesday from 10:00 a.m. to 2:00 p.m. in the Rec room located on the second floor.

SHARE THE TIME COMMITMENT IF APPLICABLE

Some leaders will use this in the job description and others won't. Some roles are seasonal such as shoveling snow from the sidewalk and throwing down salt. Others are a year round commitment such as ushering. If applicable, specify the time frame of the job.

OFFER TRAINING

Training is very important to the volunteer. It gives great peace of mind for a volunteer to know that she will knows what she is supposed to do. She will show up the first day confident. Without training, she will be apprehensive and lack confidence. Help your volunteers hit the ground running. Word will get around. When people know you train your volunteers so they can succeed from the get-go, they will want to work with you.

Have a booklet or binder made for that role. Find videos that cover certain aspects of the role. Meet with the person for lunch or in your office. Have a mentor who has done the role before serve with the newbie the first couple times to provide assurance.

VALUE STACK IT

Convey the benefits of volunteering in your ministry or organization. If you're a Christian leader, a part of a Christian ministry, there ought to be some Christian benefits. Mention the spiritual, intangible, eternal things at stake. What about practical things? Like having great coffee and serving doughnuts and fruit! Another benefit is that of community. They're going to be part of a close-knit community of other volunteers.

Now, here's the thing. When you create a job description as part of your plan for having a volunteer breakthrough, this needs to be one sheet or less. Now, don't go size 6 font or type so you can get it all on one sheet. Use short paragraphs and bullet points to add variety to your job description.

SCREEN YOUR VOLUNTEERS

In the world we live in, part of the plan must include background checks (screenings). Especially if your organization involves working with children, young people, and/or families, you have to screen your volunteers. Not only for the safety of the children and the young people, but for your safety as a leader and for the overall safety and liability of the organization that you represent. Fortunately it's easier today with the Internet. There are a lot of websites that, for a minimal fee, can screen your volunteers. My friend, Craig Jutila was the children's pastor at Saddleback Church for many years. He said, "In God we trust. Everyone else we screen." Screen everyone.

This is important, yet difficult to carry out: Don't grandfather people in. Explain that there is new policy – which there is because you are creating it. You want to set the bar high and protect everyone involved, including the volunteer. You also want to protect the church or organization. If someone gets bent out of shape bad enough because you're going to screen him and he quits, maybe there's a reason he's mad and quit. Maybe he shouldn't be volunteering after all. Please, screen everyone in your ministry, yourself included.

PLAN FOR GROWTH

My friend Jim Wideman tells leaders to run your ministry like it's twice its size. He goes on to say that if you do when you're small what you will be forced to do when you're big, you will get big.

I wonder sometimes if God looks down from heaven and sees leaders He wants to bless with growth, but they're not prepared for the growth, so He passes that blessing on to someone else. I want to be prepared for growth. So you know what? Part of my identifying the volunteer positions that I need is not just the ministry needs I have today. I look down the road to the ministry positions I need as if we are twice the size.

FINAL THOUGHT

What are some takeaways for you? Go to your Game Plan and write down what you need to do. Have you identified your current positions? Do you have job descriptions for all your positions? What about thinking ahead, being a visionary leader, being a forward thinking leader? Have you identified future positions?

MY GAME PLAN

THE LAW OF THE ASK

I'M VERY EXCITED ABOUT THIS chapter because this is vitally important. You can have everything else right. You can study people. You can even have great people skills. You can have a vision for what your ministry or organization is to become. You can even have a solid plan in place. But if you never get out and start talking to people, it's like you have a brand new, state of the art football stadium but no football team.

Jesus asked people. He asked men to follow Him. He said He would make them fishers of men. It was such a compelling ask that those early disciples left their nets behind. They left their families behind. They didn't look back. It was a high calling. So He made a pretty big ask, and He got some significant response. There comes a point where you have to begin asking for help.

ASK GOD

First, you need to ask God. What does scripture say? A few references come to mind, like James 4:2. You have not because you ask not. That's very significant, especially when you work with volunteers and have a lot of positions. Maybe there were some people who would have served with you, but you never talked to God about it. You have not because you ask not.

What about this one: Matthew 16:18? Those of you who are church leaders and ministers like this verse. Jesus said that He would build His church. You don't need to build His church. He will. He went on to say that we need to pray to the Lord of the harvest and that He would send workers into the harvest.

There was a time when I, as a young pastor, was short on help and I didn't know what to do except to vent. There was an older man who was one of my junior church volunteers. I told him I didn't know what to do. He said, "Have you prayed about it?" Light bulb! I said, "You know what? I haven't." And he quoted Matthew 16:18 to me. We need to work like it's all on us, and pray and act by faith, because it's all on the Lord. Ask God.

Too often prayer becomes the last ditch effort. You try everything else and when nothing happens, then you think, *Maybe I should pray.* But praying should have been the very first thing you did! We are all guilty of this.

ASK PEOPLE

Ask God. Then ask people.

People are full of excuses. Some good, some bad, some legitimate. Some people just simply have excuses, and their priorities are out of whack. But this is where you build a relationship, going back to Law No. 2, the law of recruiting. You build a relationship with people. And then cast the vision (Law No. 3). And before long, those excuses go away.

Now, I know, especially if you're in church work, you shouldn't have to ask people to serve. They should be willing to serve, and they should be jumping in. They should tackle the pastors in the hallway, asking how they can help. The reality is that 99% of people aren't going to do that, but there are people who will serve when they are asked.

Think back to Law No. 1 – human needs. People need to be needed. How well do you communicate to people that you have a need for them? There is a natural human trigger that occurs when people are asked to fill a significant role – when they know they are needed.

One of the biggest obstacles that you have when recruiting people is your desk. You spend way too much time at your desk, way too much time in your office. Here's the thing. Volunteers aren't going to line up outside your door. You have to go out and build relationships with people. It's about relationships.

Stop and think about it: Did God sit and wait for volunteers? He sent a burning bush to Moses. He sent a big whale to Jonah. He sent a blinding light to Saul. So if God didn't sit back and wait on volunteers, neither should you. Ask God, and then ask people.

MAKE THE BIG ASK

When we think about the law of the ask, I want to challenge you with something that Bill Hybels at Willow Creek challenged me on, and that is not to ever be afraid to make the big ask. He talks about this in his book, *Axiom*. There were times when he wanted to go after someone to join the staff, but he thought there was no way the person would say yes. But he went ahead and made the big ask. And there were times when the person said yes.

So think through it as a volunteer leader. You might think, *I have no paid staff. I sure wish I had an administrative assistant, but how would anybody ever volunteer 20 hours a week for me?* That's a big ask. But there are people who will respond to a big ask. So don't be afraid to do it. Maybe you want to start a new program, but you don't know if that person would be up for the task. Talk to God about it, and then make the big ask. For some of you, this could be a game changer if you would get out of your comfort zone and start making the big ask.

FINAL THOUGHT

Go to your Game Plan. What are two things in particular that you need to do? Do you ask God to provide the help you need? Maybe what you need to do is get a prayer journal and start praying for people. Maybe God has put some people on your heart that you think can serve. Instead of just keeping it up in your head, put it in your prayer journal and start praying for those people.

Maybe one of your big takeaways is that you're spending too much time behind your desk when you really need to get out and be with people. Maybe you need to designate a half a day a week or 30 minutes a day where you are intentional about building relationships so that you can begin asking people to do what they've been called to do.

Maybe every one of your serving opportunities looks the same way: Every week for life or every other month till Jesus comes. Or maybe you're short-term. All you do is ask for the short-term, and you need to create some long-term opportunities to keep people engaged. Maybe this needs to be part of your personal strategy.

Before you read any further, write down a few takeaways. Begin putting these into practice TODAY.

MY GAME PLAN

_____

_____

_____

_____

_____

_____

_____

_____

_____

_____

_____

_____

_____

_____

_____

_____

_____

_____

_____

_____

_____

_____

_____

_____

THE LAW OF BEST FIT

THERE IS NOTHING FUN ABOUT having a volunteer come up to you and say he's burned out or tired. And there's nothing exciting about having a new volunteer, disappear after two weeks.

When someone says she's burned out, she's saying there is a need in her life that is not being met. Volunteers won't say that, but that's what they're saying. And sometimes – not always, but sometimes – when a volunteer comes to you and says, "I'm burned out," it could very well be that where she is serving that does not fit with her gifts and/or the point where she's at in her life.

Many times it can mean that there is some other need that's not being met, and it may be totally unrelated to you or your organization or ministry context. But there is nothing fun about a volunteer who's burned out. Or like I said earlier, you get that volunteer, you put him in a room, you give him a responsibility, he lasts a few weeks or even a few months and then, poof. Gone.

I'm going to recommend this book to you: Jim Collins' classic book, *Good to Great*. By the way, he has a smaller version of this book that is specifically for nonprofits. They're both very good books. The point of the book is that, according to his analytics, great companies are those that put the right people on the bus, to use his terminology. The bus takes them where they need to go, and great companies make sure they have the right people on the bus. This brings up two poignant questions: Do you have the right people on the bus; and are those people in the right seats?

QUESTION 1: DO YOU HAVE THE RIGHT PEOPLE ON THE BUS

In the book *Good to Great*, Collins talks about getting the right people on the bus. Question: do you feel like you have the right people on the bus?

Who are the right people? That's where you have to start. Who is it that you are trying to target? Who are you trying to go after in your ministry? Who is the target? Who is the bull's-eye? Let me give you a few things you need to look for.

LOOK AT YOUR CURRENT AND FUTURE NEEDS

So as you think about the bull's-eye, the right people, what are you current needs? If you need a teacher, that's the right person for the bus right now. If you need a behind-the-scenes person, that's the right person for the bus right now.

Then look at your future needs. This goes back to Law No. 4, the law of the plan. What is it that you need in the future? What kinds of people and positions will you need? You need to make sure you have those people on the bus because they are who you project you will need.

DETERMINE WHO YOU WANT TO REACH

Who you want to reach will determine who the right people are for the bus. If you're trying to reach senior citizens, having a teenager or college student may not be the most effective. It might because there are some younger people who have hearts for the elderly and are received well by them. But, in general, a really young person might not be the right person. If you're trying to reach teenagers and communicate effectively, you want to make sure you have someone who can communicate to them effectively. You have to know the feel and personality of the teens and that will direct you to the right person to put on the bus.

IDENTIFY WHO YOU WOULD LIKE TO CLONE

You should always be duplicating yourself and duplicating the bright stars, key people on your team. Who is it that you want to clone? What are characteristics about them that you want to find in other potential volunteers?

I tell my people all the time, "You should always be working yourself out of a job." Always work yourself out of a job and get someone else to do what you're doing. So who do you want to clone?

QUESTION 2: ARE THEY IN THE RIGHT SEATS ON THE BUS?

You can have the bus in motion and have the right people on the bus, but have them in the wrong seats. Not everyone has the license to drive a bus. Not everyone should be sitting in the back of the bus. Some people get carsick. Not everyone has the patience to be the monitor who walks up and down the bus. So practically, you can have the right people. They can have the right traits and characteristics. They can even meet your current and future needs. But where are you going to put them?

DISCOVER THE BEST FIT FOR YOUR VOLUNTEERS

It takes time to get to know your volunteers but you need to assess their traits and abilities early on. There are so many options available online. There are tests that help people identify their gifts, strengths, and abilities. Then you can line those up with the needs you have within your organization. Taking this step will save frustration on the part of volunteers because you are setting them up to succeed. And it's also going to be less frustration for the people who those volunteer are working for or with because these volunteers are all in sync. It's miserable working with someone who is out of sync. God has wired each of us differently, so you need to assess your volunteers to see where they fit best.

UNDERSTAND THE PERSONAL PREFERENCES OF YOUR VOLUNTEERS

Ask your volunteers what they believe to be their gifts, talents, and abilities, and then discover their preferences. Some people are very task oriented. Others are very people oriented. Some people are up-front types. They're very comfortable and enjoy talking in front of others. Other people are behind-the-scenes types. Some people like to do the same thing every week. Some people want variety in what they do. Take time to discover people's preferences and do your best to accommodate them, given that their preferences are in line with their skills and the needs of your ministry or organization.

FINAL THOUGHT

Go to your Game Plan and consider these questions: Do you have the right people on the bus? If yes, are they in the right seats? If no, what will you do, even today, to start addressing the situation? Maybe your answer is both yes and no. Some of the people on the bus are the right people but others aren't. Don't go to the next chapter until you wrestle with these questions for a bit. Having the right people in the right places can make or break a ministry or organization.

MY GAME PLAN

THE LAW OF TRAINING

WHEN I WROTE MY FIRST book, *9 Things They Didn't Teach Me in College About Children's Ministry*, I devoted an entire chapter to how we train volunteers in the local church. And I did some research on the amount of effort, both time and resources, that Starbucks puts into training an employee how to make a cup of coffee. It's an extensive amount of training to get that cup of coffee just right.

But so often in church and nonprofit work, we sign people up and throw them into a room with very little training, if any. The gospel ministry is so much more significant than serving a cup of coffee. It's essential to train volunteers. It sets both you and them up for success.

WHEN VOLUNTEERS ARE NOT TRAINED

So what happens when you don't train a volunteer? It's disheartening and confusing for everyone involved.

NO TRAINING = POOR PERFORMANCE

First of all, you're going to find that you have poor performance. Why is that person doing such a lousy job? Well, you know what? They weren't trained. This is why Starbucks spends so much money training their baristas how to make the perfect latte. They want to make sure that you get a great beverage. If you want your volunteers to perform with excellence, you have to make sure that they are trained. When you don't train, performance will be poor.

NO TRAINING = PEOPLE DON'T UNDERSTAND THE BOUNDARIES

Why on earth did that person do that? She was never told she couldn't do that. Well, what makes Jim think he has the authority to make that decision? Well, he was never told any differently. Do you see what I'm saying here? If volunteers aren't told what they can should and should not do, you can't be mad at them. It ultimately comes back to you.

NO TRAINING = PEOPLE WILL FEEL LOST

Volunteers will feel lost when there is no training. When you put them in a room with no training, they will be uncertain. They need to know whom they go to should they need help where they can find the resources they need, whether they can spend money, or if they have the power to make certain decisions.

NO TRAINING = PEOPLE QUIT

This is what can happen when you have a volunteer who hasn't been trained. He'll quit on you. I have some success stories in my ministry only by God's grace, but I have a lot more failure stories than success stories. This is one reason the KidzMatter magazine has a section called the Oops File. We share oops stories so we can learn from our mistakes. I've learned that if you throw a warm body in a room and give him a task without training, chances are he's going to quit. Volunteers are precious and valuable. We need to treat them with respect and honor their decision to serve the ministry or organization. Train them and you'll retain them.

NO TRAINING = PEOPLE HAVE NEGATIVE EXPERIENCES

When volunteers have a negative experience, they will probably share it with others. People don't want to serve where they don't feel valued and when they don't know what they're supposed to do and don't have the confidence to do their task, they will tell others so their friends and family don't have the same negative experience. As a result, it undermines the very integrity and reputation or brand of your ministry or organization.

Of course you don't want your volunteers to quit or have negatives experiences. But when they don't have the tools and resources and knowledge to do their job, they will have negative experiences.

When your volunteers are trained, they are fired up, passionate, and engaged. And they find deep fulfillment. And you find fulfillment. Ephesians 4:11-12 says that, as a leader, one of your tasks is to equip others to do the work of the ministry.

THREE STYLES OF LEARNING

Now, before we really dig into what people need to be trained on and how you go about training people in today's economy of time, I want to talk about how people learn. There are different approaches to how people learn. I often refer to Marlene LeFever's classic book, *Learning Styles* published by David C Cook. It's an older book, but it's great. She identifies the four main learning styles of people.

I also like to reference Marcus Buckingham's approach in his book *The One Thing You Need to Know*. He takes people and classifies them into three learning styles. By and large, most people fit into one of the following three categories.

THE ANALYZER

The analyzer is the observer. The analyzer is the one who wants to learn from a mentor. He wants to watch and read and study. The analyzer is great in the aspect that when he show up for the job, he's super prepared. Why? Because he has done the research. He has done his homework. He has asked questions.

Now, the downside to an analyzer: You don't throw an analyzer into a room without allowing him to be prepared. If you do he'll freak out. He may try to wing it for you, but he's not going to be happy, and he's not going to stick around for the long haul. The analyzer is a student, so consequently he wants to know what he's getting into. By the way, your analyzer likes to meet and discuss things. The more prepared he feels, the better he'll perform.

Look at Thomas from the New Testament. He was an analyzer. Remember when Jesus appeared in his post-resurrection body, Thomas wanted to see if it was Jesus. He wanted to touch his hands. Sometimes we get on Thomas as being the doubter. Well, it wasn't that Thomas was a faithless man. It was his learning style. He was an analyzer. He needed to see it. He needed to touch it. He needed to feel it. Some people are analyzers. The analyzer does things in a ready, aim, fire order.

THE DOER

The doer doesn't want to study. She doesn't want to analyze, scrutinize, meet, or discuss. In fact, she'll just go and make it happen. She learns by doing. The analyzer learns by studying. The doer learns by doing. She's going to learn by practical experience. She doesn't need to sit through a class to learn how to do something – at least she doesn't think she needs to. She doesn't want a manual. She doesn't want to take your course or sit through pre-launch training. She just wants to do it.

Peter was a doer. When Jesus walked up to the disciples on the water, Peter was the one who wanted to walk out to him. No thinking. Just doing. So he got out of the boat and started walking. But when he started thinking, he started sinking. Sometimes we get on Peter for his lack of faith. But he stepped out of the boat to begin with, right? He was willing to do something.

Your doer wants to go right to work. Her motto in life is ready, fire, aim. She fires before she aims.

THE WATCHER

The third learning style is the watcher. The watcher learns by observing and watching. The watcher needs to have a mentor that he follows and learns from.

If you have recruited a new volunteer and his learning style is the watcher, you need to assign a more seasoned volunteer to spend some time with him. That watcher needs to shadow someone.

IDENTIFYING YOUR VOLUNTEERS' LEARNING STYLES

Do you know the learning styles of your current volunteers? Could you write down their names and learning style? If not, you need to find out what they are. There are various learning style assessments that can be found Online. Taking this step will save you and your volunteers some frustration. And it will help you as you recruit new volunteers. When your volunteers training and have continued training that addresses their learning style, they will be more engaged and excited and confident.

HOW TO TRAIN YOUR VOLUNTEERS

Early in my ministry, I inherited a monthly worker's meeting. The first Sunday of every month, all the children's ministry workers came to church early for a meeting. Most everyone would show up. We had doughnuts and drinks and shared announcements. And we had a short training session. People felt connected and encouraged.

But we don't do that anymore. Why? Because, used alone, it stopped working. Can you imagine if you tried to get all of your volunteers to come to a monthly meeting and this was the only training you provided? You would get some, but not all of them, right? People are busy and their priorities are in different places. Now, should their priorities be in training? Perhaps. But the reality is their priorities are in different places so in may churches, a monthly training session isn't logical.

But, when it's used in conjunction with other forms of training it still have value – especially for your analyzers.

So, then, how do you train volunteers?

SHOTGUN APPROACH

When I'm talking to leaders of nonprofits and churches, I love to ask them what they do to train their volunteers. One of the things I hear over and over again from leaders who train volunteers is that they do a little bit of everything. It's what I refer to as the shotgun approach. The shotgun approach affirms that there is not one way to train volunteers. You have to go at it multiple ways. Kind of like when you shoot a shotgun. That bullet spreads out.

Practically, the shot gun approach looks like this: there a various options and methods of training. There are meetings, there's a Facebook group, there are email blasts, and podcasts. There are various ways to dispense the training so that people can find a way that engages them and works into their schedule.

Do you see where I'm going with the shotgun approach? Is it going to take work? Yes. But it's one of the greatest investments you can make. You will never regret this kind of investment. It's something you can do to pour into other volunteers and help them go further faster. And consider this, once you find your methods, times, establish templates, etc., the time to send out the information will decrease.

TYPES OF TRAINING

There's how to train your volunteers, and then there's what your volunteers need to be trained in. Your volunteers need to be trained in two areas.

First, they need to be trained in organizational-specific things. This is the wider area. They need to understand the mission and vision of the ministry or organization? They need to know the chain of command and the organizational chart.

Second, they need job-specific training. If you've recruited a volunteer to serve in the food pantry or to teach a class or drive a bus, she also needs job-specific training. In this training she will learn exactly what is expected of her and how she can do it.

Here's where training often falls short. Sometimes training is focused on only one of these two areas instead of both. Or there's no training at all. Volunteers need to be trained and they need to be fully trained.

TRAINING PREVENTS BURNOUT

Training is one of the best ways to avoid burnout. When you train your volunteers, not only on the front end, but when you provide continual training opportunities, you help them avoid burnout. Continued training provides encouragement and reassurance. It rekindles the fire the volunteer felt when she first started serving. Especially if a volunteer is going through some difficult things at home or work or even in her ministry role, training and being with other volunteers bolsters the heart and soul. It reminds her that she's not alone.

Elijah needed to be reminded that he wasn't alone. After his victory on Mount Caramel, when the prophets of Baal were humiliated, Queen Jezebel was furious and wanted Elijah dead because he refused to bow to Baal. So he ran and ran. At one point he rested under a tree and begged God to take his life. He was scared and tired. But God reminded him that he wasn't alone. There were hundreds of other people who also refused to bow to Baal. Once he realized he wasn't alone, he was able to stand up and do battle for God.

When your volunteers receive continued training and support, they will feel encouraged and energized. They'll remember that they're not alone in their work and will continue to serve with passion.

FINAL THOUGHT

Before you jump into the next chapter, record some of your takeaways in your Game Plan. Do you know the learning style of your volunteers? How will you go about learning them and what will you do with that knowledge?

Are you training effectively?

Maybe one of your takeaways is that you need to begin using the shotgun approach to training. You might need to schedule two hours a week to do nothing but train. It could be a different thing every week. Or it might be the same things at a set time every week, like doing a podcast or an email newsletter. The first step is to choose to do it and decide when and what. But you need to schedule it. Again, it's an investment of time, but it is one of the greatest investments you can make. If for no other reason, it will help people avoid burnout and have a sense of fulfillment in what they are doing.

Feel like you don't have the budget to do this? Burn that excuse. If you don't have a budget line, create one. If you can't afford a microphone to create a podcast, take budget money from somewhere else or reach out to people in the church who have the gift of sharing their money and resources and ask for help. There are a host of website providers where you can create a website for very little or at no cost. Find ways to push past barriers. You, your volunteers, and your ministry or organization will be better for your efforts.

MY GAME PLAN

_____

_____

_____

_____

_____

_____

_____

_____

_____

_____

_____

_____

_____

_____

_____

_____

_____

_____

_____

_____

_____

_____

_____

_____

_____

_____

_____

_____

_____

_____

_____

_____

_____

_____

_____

_____

_____

_____

_____

_____

_____

_____

_____

_____

_____

_____

_____

_____

_____

_____

LAW 8

THE LAW OF EXCELLENCE

YOU'LL WANT TO BOOKMARK THE GAME PLAN pages at the end of this chapter because you'll want to write notes while you read. I'm praying that the Lord will bring some things to your mind and will challenge your thinking about excellence and it has to do with recruiting and keeping volunteers.

We refer to restaurants and athletes as being excellent. But what does it mean? I can't take the credit for what I'm going to share with you here. I first heard this from my coach and mentor, Jim Wideman. Together, we've wrestled with what excellence looks like in leadership. He always starts by talking about what excellence is not. Excellence is not just about winning. The excellent athlete is not necessarily the one who wins. The excellent investor does not always get the highest return at the end of the day. There's more to being excellent than winning.

EXCELLENCE REQUIRES THAT YOU STRIVE TO BE BETTER

Are you striving to be a better leader than you were last week, last month, last year? Are you striving to grow in your interpersonal skills? Are you striving to be a better communicator than you were at your last event? Are you learning new techniques?

Here's the beauty of excellence. Excellence is the very road that takes you to a successful life. If you want to have success in your life and ministry, excellence is will get you there.

Stop and think about people you know who have been committed to excellence. Think about sports. I think of Michael Jordan or Peyton Manning. They have demonstrated excellence in sports. What about in acting? I think of Audrey Hepburn or Harrison Ford. What about in business? In business, I think of guys like Steve Jobs or Bill Gates. If you go back a little further than that, think about Andrew Carnegie or Dale Carnegie in business and leadership. Also think about people you know personally who demonstrate excellence.

It's good to think on people who model excellence and choose characteristics and aspects to emulate. Read what they write. Listen intently and learn from what they say. I may not have a personal relationship with some of them, but I'm going to learn from them however I can. Excellence is demonstrated all around us. Seek it out and it will happen for you.

I kind of feel like I'm preaching to the choir here because I'm talking to someone who has taken a deeper step and wants to get more intensive in his or her learning. You've joined this coaching class. You've put some money on the table. You've invested your time. You have a commitment to excellence or you wouldn't be reading this book. You wouldn't be this far along in this course with me making up a game plan for how to get better at recruiting and keeping volunteers. You're well on your way, but I'm praying this book will stir a desire for you to raise the bar of excellence higher.

This is not only a good thing. It's a smart thing. It's a biblical thing. In Colossians 3:17, God says, "And whatever you do, in word or deed, do everything in the name of the Lord Jesus, giving thanks to God the Father through him." *Whatever* you do.

Those of you who have heard the KidzMatter story, you know that God has continued to bless our ministry. It was born out of our local church ministry. The very building I spend the majority of my works days in was given to our ministry by the Green family, owners of Hobby Lobby. Very providentially about four years ago, I was introduced to the Green family. I was able to share the vision for our ministry and how God has blessed and how we're careful to give Him the praise. They wanted to know about some specific needs. At the time, we really needed space. By God's hand, we found a building that was a good fit for our current and future needs. God chose to use the Green family to buy that building as a gift to our ministry.

A year or two back I did an interview with Steve Green, founder and still the active president of Hobby Lobby. Our magazine is primarily for people in children's and family ministry so many of our readers shop at Hobby Lobby – especially when it's time for VBS or summer camp!

At the end of our interview, Steve said this to me, "I learned from my dad a long time ago that anything done in the name of the Lord should be done with excellence." He has definitely demonstrated that in his life. You need to read his story if you've it. I appreciate the stand that he has made for the Lord and how he's attempted to honor the Lord in his business.

EXCELLENCE ATTRACTS EXCELLENCE

What does excellence have to do with recruiting and keeping volunteers? It has everything to do with it, because excellence attracts excellence. Excellent employers attract excellent employees. Excellent leaders attract excellent followers. Excellent nonprofits attract excellent donors.

And the opposite is also true. A lack of excellence attracts a lack of excellence. If the leaders are not committed to excellence, they're going to attract followers and volunteers who aren't committed to excellence. People who lead programs and are always winging it and doing it half-heartedly are going to attract volunteers who go at it the same way. If you're going to have a volunteer breakthrough like never before, this is critical. You have to be committed to excellence.

It doesn't matter if you have a limited budget because excellence does not mean extravagance. You can do excellence on a shoestring budget because excellence doesn't mean you're the best. Excellence doesn't have to mean you have the most money to spend. Excellence doesn't have to mean you have the shiniest new gadget. Excellence means you're doing things better than you've ever done them before. You are a mode of constant improvement and want to consistently get better because you understand that it is the very road that leads to success in life and ministry.

Here are some ways you can achieve excellence.

LEAD YOURSELF

You have to learn how to lead yourself. It doesn't mean that you don't place yourself under authority or under leadership or that you're a lone ranger out doing your own thing. No. It means that you're not relying on other people to lead you and help you be better. You're doing it yourself.

Think about whom you spend the most time with in a given day. Spouse, boss, co-worker, someone you share the cubicle with. Do you know who you spend the most time with in a given day? Yourself. The best person to lead you and push you to be more growth oriented is you. Don't be over dependent on someone else to lead you toward excellence. Lead yourself to it.

In I Samuel 30:6, David encouraged himself in the Lord. King Saul was chasing him, but David encouraged himself in the Lord. It's not your boss' job to encourage you. It's not your pastor's job to encourage you. It's not your husband's job, or your wife's job. David encouraged himself in the Lord. He led himself. So be committed to leading yourself. Make personal development a priority in your life.

Go to your Game Plan and write this down: I need to make personal development a priority. I need to devote X number of hours a week to learning and growing myself. I need to spend time in God's Word. I need to spend time listening to God's Word being taught. I need to learn from other leaders. I need to be reading. I need to be listening to blogs. I need to make this a priority.

ALWAYS SEEK TO IMPROVE

Never be content with how things are. The routine should never be the routine because that means you're not growing and improving. Athletes have coaches and trainers and will record their games so they can watch the video and learn from it. If athletes are constantly trying to improve, how does this translate to your ministry or organization? What are you doing to constantly improve?

Are you self-evaluating? I would encourage you to self-evaluate. Take time and ask yourself how you're doing. There are ways you can do this. One is to ask people you trust for their feedback. Maybe it's your assistant. Maybe it's your spouse. Maybe it's your boss. You want them to be honest; so don't get upset when they share areas where you can improve. In the context of your work or organization, take closer consideration of your annual evaluation. Don't glance at it and file it. Read and digest it. Maybe you need to just figure it out yourself. If you're a communicator, maybe you need to record yourself communicating, watch it, as painful as that can be, and critique yourself.

Be in a constant mode of improvement. Remember, this is what excellence is – it's striving to be better than you used to be. So if you want to achieve excellence, you not only need to learn to lead yourself, but you also need to seek to improve. The routine should never be the routine.

AVOID THE TYRANNY OF THE URGENT

There's a book I love to recommend to people. It's called *Tyranny of the Urgent* by Charles Hummel. I buy them and give them away all the time because one of the greatest dangers that you have as a leader, one of the greatest threats to excellence, is to allow urgent things to trump critical things. There's a big difference between things that are urgent and things that are critical.

There is great tension that resides between how you decide between the urgent and the critical. Here's an example of the urgent: your email inbox. Someone emails and says that something needs to be done ASAP. Then the phone rings. You need to take the phone call. Someone walks in your office and needs to talk. These are urgent things that come up.

Critical things are those that only you can do that move the vision, the mission, the values, and the direction of your organization forward. These are things that trump urgent things. The problem is that if you're not strategic and intentional, you will always allow the urgent things to trump the critical things. So you will get to the end of the week and realize that all you did was put out fires. You caved to the tyranny, the craziness of the urgent. However, if you choose what you're going to focus on, the critical things, all of a sudden you can get done what needs to get done.

Think about Jesus. Think about all the pressures that were on Him. Yet toward the end of His earthly ministry, He prayed to the Father saying, "I've done what you have called me to do" (paraphrase). How could he say that? There were still people who need to be healed and saved and fed. But Jesus was saying that He did what God had instructed Him to do, not what everyone was demanding that He needed to do.

ESTABLISH STRUCTURE

This ties right into the tyranny of the urgent. What is your structure? What is your 24/7? I'll tell you this. You need to have a daily structure. Now, I know that in leadership, things change. There are certain demands at certain given times of the year and certain days of the week. But by and large, you need to have structure in your life. You need to be structured for growth.

Let me give you a few tips.

One way to establish structure in your life is to not check your email the first hour of the day. I used to check my email first thing when I woke up and then first thing when I got into the office. I don't do that anymore. I do not check my email until I've been in the office for at least one hour. So it actually ends up being two or three hours into my day. Why? Because if I check my email the first thing every day, other people are going to dictate to me what I'm going to do. My email inbox simply becomes a to-do list that other people are pushing on me. So am I going to live based upon the dictates of other people, or am I going to control my schedule and have structure? If you want structure, the one way to set it is not to check your email the first hour of the day.

And I would encourage you with this thought. Don't do anything digital the first or last hour of the day, but especially the last. When you can disconnect digitally the last hour of the day, you will sleep better. You will wake up more refreshed. You will be able to focus your mind the last hour of the day on things that you need to focus on, not things other people are feeding you.

One of the first things I do when I get to the office is determine what I want to get done that day, and I use what I call my productivity playbook. It's simply a one-page sheet that I've created that includes things that I have to get done today no matter what and people I need to talk to in order to move a project forward. Then I list a few big projects I have happening so that if I get those other things done, there are some things that I can do to move some of these projects forward. I make a new productivity planner every day and that determines what I am going to do that day no matter what.

Some people ask me, how I get so much stuff done. I'm a pastor, lead a nonprofit, am an entrepreneur, publish a magazine, and have a family. Here's the thing: I have established structure. Now, I don't always get it right. And, yes, I get stressed now and then, and the demands feel very heavy. And I have to say "yes" and "no," and some days my priority planner goes out the window because of a certain phone call or project. But overall, I set the tone and structure for the day and am able to achieve what I have planned.

Figure out what do you need to do in order to create structure. Why? So you can have excellence in your life and ministry. Why? Because excellence attracts excellence, which can lead to a volunteer breakthrough like never before.

FINAL THOUGHT

If you're going to seek excellence, seek it in all areas of life. How's your walk with God? If you're a Christian leader, that needs to be priority No. 1, right? Are you pursuing excellence in your walk with God? Are you closer to God today than you were last week, or have you drifted? By the way, if you're not intentional, you'll drift. We were in Florida for vacation and took the girls to the beach. I waded out and after 10 minutes I looked back and couldn't find Beth. I had drifted without even knowing it. If you're not intentional about growing spiritually, you will drift.

What about at home? I love helping you be a better leader, but there is something more important than my wife and kids. I've learned this: my wife could care less how many people follow me on Twitter. She loves me, she supports me, but she doesn't care. She doesn't follow that. My girls are probably never going to read my resume. But you know what? What God has called me to do at home trumps everything else.

So seek excellence in all areas: in my your with God, at home, at work, in your recreation, in your health.

Go to your Game Plan. What do you need to do differently or what do you need to start doing to raise the bar of excellence in your ministry? Now do it.

MY GAME PLAN

THE LAW OF APPRECIATION

IF YOU'RE A NONPROFIT OR church leader, your greatest treasures are your volunteers. They give you their time, effort, and energy. Even just an hour a week of someone's time is very precious. You need to show appreciation to your volunteers.

The truth is that we all need to be appreciated. It goes back to one of those basic human needs in Law No. 1, the need to be appreciated. God wired us this way. At home, I have a file cabinet. In those files, I keep all of our home, business, and financial stuff. I have a file in there that I started back when I was a teenager. I've kept all the significant letters and cards and things that I've received in the mail through the years. Maybe you have something like this at home.

I was rummaging through that file cabinet a while back, trying to find something, and I came across that file. It had been a while since I looked through it and I found some really neat things that people have given me over the years. And the majority of them were notes of appreciation or words of affirmation.

I have a letter from my pastor who wrote me after the first time I was able to preach at church as a teen. I have an appreciation letter from Art Rorheim, the founder of Awana. Beth's grandfather, who's gone home to be with the Lord, was a pastor. He wrote me a note after I sang in church one time.

I could go on and on telling you about stuff that's in that folder, but the point is that we are wired in such a way that when someone takes time to show us gratitude or appreciation, it means a lot to us. If you're going to keep volunteers for the long haul, you have to show them that you appreciate them. After all, they're not getting a pay check or any health or retirement benefits.

Everyone needs to feel appreciated. It motivates them to press on when they're frustrated and reminds them of their value. Here are some ways to show your volunteers how much you value and appreciate them.

GIVE THEM TIME

Do for one what you wish you could do for all. Andy Stanley teaches that, and it's a great principle. Maybe you can't take all of your volunteers to lunch, but you can take one of them to lunch. Maybe you can't take them all for coffee this week, but you can take one. Maybe you don't have time to give every one of them a call today, but you can call one each day.

Do for one what you wish you could do for all. Volunteers desperately need your time.

GIVE THEM THANKS

Volunteers need to hear "thank you." Almost every day of the week I send a thank you card to someone. Why? Because it goes a long way. It's refreshing to go out to the mailbox and find something other than a bill and junk mail. When people get a thank you note in the mail and it's a thank you card, it can change their whole day.

Gift cards to Starbucks or Dunkin' Donuts go a long way too. Cards don't have to be more than $5 for someone to feel appreciated. Let me just say this: cut the I-don't-have-any-money excuse. One time I challenged a group of people to give gift cards and everyone said, "But I don't have a budget." Your volunteers are giving you hours of their time. If you really value them, you're going to find $5 somewhere. Now, I know you might not have thousands of dollars to spend, but I bet you can find $5 a week.

Sometimes it's as simple as going up to someone, shaking his hand and saying "thanks." When is the last time someone told you thanks? It's a rare commodity, isn't it? But because it's a rare commodity, it is of great value. Your volunteers will remember the time you sent them a note or gift card or took a few minutes to share some coffee. It bolsters their enthusiasm and encourages them to continue in their service.

GIVE THEM BREAKS

Everyone needs a break now and then. Baseball players play about 160 games a year. That's a lot of games. But they take a season break, which is crucial to recovering and then preparing for the next season. There are times when your volunteers need a break, and one of the greatest ways you can show them appreciation is by offering them a break. See if they need to take a couple weeks off. They will come back, but that break shows them appreciation.

GIVE THEM RECOGNITION

Consider starting a volunteer of the month feature. I used to have a volunteer of the month. The volunteer had a special parking spot at church and his/her name went up on a plaque. We gave the volunteers public recognition. Another option is to recognize volunteers based on the n umber of years they've served. Have one-year, five-year, etc. awards and make them a big deal. Hand out a nice certificate and gift.

Instead of a $5 gift card, step up your game and invest $20 or $30 gift card. Or maybe it's a babysitting night for your volunteers. Tell your volunteers to bring their kids to church and you're going to provide babysitting so the volunteers and their significant other can have a night out. Or send them to special training. If there's a conference in the area that would benefit your volunteers, send them. You'll benefit from what they learn too!

Take pictures of all your volunteers and have them scrolling on a TV in a high traffic area. When others pass by, they can see who is on your team.

Something else volunteers will appreciate is swag. Put your ministry, church, or organization logo on shirts, mugs, totes, key chains and randomly hand them out when your volunteers arrive to serve. Or send them a package in the mail.

Then there are the large-scale things that you can do too like appreciation events. This is something I love to do every year for my volunteers at our church. Some years we'll roast a pig, and we'll have a cowboy theme. We make it a special evening. They don't have to bring anything except themselves and their families.

Another large-scale option is an outing to take all your volunteers and their families to an amusement park or host a picnic or BBQ at a park.

When hosting these large-scale events, recognize your volunteers. This could be where you hand out service awards and swag. Help them feel like they're a big deal – because they are!

FINAL THOUGHT

If you need more volunteers, make heroes of the ones you already have. One of the best investments you can make is appreciating your volunteers. So how are you doing in this area? Go to your Game Plan and put some thoughts on paper. What do you need to do? Where and how can you step up your game?

Now think long term. Maybe you want to do some things but you don't have the budget for them right now. Next time budget planning comes around, add that as a line item.

MY GAME PLAN

_____

_____

_____

_____

_____

_____

_____

_____

_____

_____

_____

_____

_____

_____

_____

_____

_____

_____

_____

_____

_____

_____

_____

LAW 10

THE LAW OF THE SHEPHERD

VOLUNTEERS ARE LIKE GOLD TO you. You could not survive
without volunteers. For a lot of nonprofits and churches,
volunteers are the staff. They're the people who do what needs
to be done. They're gold. Are you treating them like the precious commodity they are?

We often approach ministry like it's a sprint. We rush here
and there. But it's not a sprint. It's a marathon. Sometimes
when we think of volunteers, we think of a checklist. OK, first
grade has a teacher now and so and so has agreed to drive the
bus, etc. Check and check.

But volunteers are more than the check marks we make on
our note pad. Part of working with people, especially volunteers, is shepherding them. Shepherding is biblical. Psalm 23
focuses on the fact that God is our shepherd. We need to learn
what a shepherd is and what he or she does and we need to
take on that role.

SHEPHERDING IN THE BIBLE

Jesus called himself the Good Shepherd. What does the good
shepherd do? The good shepherd lays down his life for the
sheep. Jesus ultimately did just that.

What else did Jesus say? He said, that His sheep know Him and hear His voice. And they follow Him. Do your volunteers know your voice, and are they following you? Do they have a personal relationship with you? There's a big difference between someone following you and someone showing up to fill a slot because she signed up on a clipboard. I'm talking about following you ultimately to the point of being willing to give you much more than what was originally understood. It's the volunteer saying, "I believe in you. I believe in this organization. I'm following you, if for no other reason, because I'm curious to see what you're up to next." If you're going to recruit and care for volunteers and keep them for the long haul, there are four ways you have to learn how to shepherd them.

KNOW YOUR PEOPLE

The shepherd knows his sheep. He knows their names and nuances. If you are going to shepherd people, you have to have a relationship with them. More than likely, you have a lot of volunteers. Well, that just means you have to work really, really hard at knowing as many of them as possible.

Have other people on your team, maybe it's your core team, know those volunteers and to have relationships with them as well. Surprise your volunteers by sending them a birthday card or sending their child a birthday card. "Wow, I didn't realize that he knew it was my kid's birthday!" Have a list of everyone's birthdays and anniversaries visible in your office and check it at the beginning of every week.

Once a month, have a volunteer and his or her family to your home for dinner. Or have a couple of families over at the same time. It's easier and more relaxed to get to know people on a deeper level when in someone's home.

You can't shepherd people if you don't have a relationship with them so get to know your volunteers.

DO THINGS FOR THEM

Part of shepherding volunteers is doing things for them on a practical level – acts of service. Jesus said a shepherd lays down his life for the sheep. That is the ultimate act of service. So what can you do? So much of working with volunteers is foot washing. Jesus washed His disciples' feet to demonstrate this. Too often, we think people ought to serve us when, in reality, the genuine call of a leader is to serve other people.

One thing Beth and I love are Dairy Queen ice cream cakes. She loves them so much, that occasionally I'll bring one home. Boy, does her face light up when I walk in the door with an ice cream cake! And I know what kind she likes. She likes the fudge ones. It's a simple gesture, an act of service for her. I do it because I know she likes them. Provide your volunteers with water, snacks, breaks from service, etc.

A shepherd meets needs and cares for the sheep. Do things for your volunteers.

BE ACCESSIBLE

If you want to show someone that you really care for her, you need to be accessible. If a volunteer has something going on in his life, be accessible.

When your phone rings, answer it. Whenever my cell phone rings, I always try to answer it, even if I have to say, "Can I call you back?" At least pick it up so the caller knows you are aware of his need to talk.

Answer emails in a timely manner. Replying to an email the same day says something – it says the person you are replying to is worth your time and effort. It communicates that you are a shepherd.

Be accessible – be the shepherd you would want to work for.

BE PRESENT FOR THEM

Sometimes we can be pretty good at caring for volunteers when they're there working for us. But what about the other days of the week? Do you care for them when they aren't volunteering for you? We all have times when we have difficult days. Emotional things come up, there are difficulties at work, problems with kids, problems at home, some kind of a challenge, etc. Whatever the situation is, do you know your volunteers well enough that they're comfortable coming to you? And when they do, how do you care for them during those difficult times?

You're not going to care for them if you don't have a relationship because you're not going to know what's going on in their life. See how all these work together? Knowing them, spending time with them, doing things for them, being there – these are all part of meeting their needs, showing that you care, helping them.

FINAL THOUGHT

So here's my challenge for you with this chapter: What do you need to do in order to create a care plan? I'd like for you to turn to your Game Plan and think through this. How can you do a better job caring for volunteers? How can you show your volunteers that you desire to be a shepherd to them?

How can you shepherd, care for, feed, and guide them? And whom can you recruit to help you in the process? Who on your core team has the makings of a shepherd? Work together and come up with a game plan for how you will become the shepherd your volunteers deserve.

ARE YOU READY FOR A BREAKTHROUGH?

Last Christmas our girls each received a gold coin. They looked at them like they were a Chuck E. Cheese coin, put them back inside their stockings, and went to play with their toys. I recognized the value of the coins, so I pulled out my phone and researched what an ounce of gold was going for. The girls didn't realize the precious gift they had been given. They said thanks to their Grandma, but they didn't realize what they had.

Your volunteers are gold. Do you treat them that way? Do you know what you have in them? While it's a great challenge, there is nothing as powerful as volunteers who have bought into the vision, who believe in you and your ministry, and want to go with you all the way to the finish line. There is tremendous value in that.

Recognize the law of human needs. Understand how to effectively recruit volunteers and convey your vision to them. Develop a plan based on your vision and then ask for help. As new volunteers join your team, make sure they're in the right seats on the bus and give them the training they need to succeed and excel in their roles. Make sure that you continually strive for excellence in everything you do. Show your volunteers that they are appreciated and shepherd, love, and care for them.

Are you ready to have a great volunteer breakthrough? Put this book into practice. Be the leader and shepherd you would want to serve.

MY GAME PLAN

RESOURCES REFERENCED THROUGHOUT THE BOOK

Buckingham, Marcus. *One Thing You Need To Know: About Great Managing, Great Leading, and Sustained Individual Success.* New York: Free Press. 2005. Print.

Carnegie, Dale. *How To Win Friends and Influence People.* Rice, WA: Cornerstone Publishing. 1937, 2005. Print.

Collins, Jim. *Good to Great: Why Some Companies Make the Leap and Others Don't.* New York: Harper Collins. 2001. Print.

Frank, Ryan. *9 Things They Didn't Teach Me In College About Children's Ministry.* Colorado Springs: Standard Publishing, 2011. Print.

The Holy Bible, English Standard Version (ESV). Wheaton: Crossway. 2011. Print.

Hummel, Charles E. *Tyranny of the Urgent.* Downers Grove, IL: Inter-Varsity Press. 1967, 1994. Print.

Hybels, Bill. *Leadership Axioms.* Grand Rapids: Zondervan. 2008. Print.

LeFever, Marlene. *Learning Styles: Reaching Everyone God Gave You To Teach.* Colorado Springs: David C. Cook. 1995, 2004. Print.

CPSIA information can be obtained
at www.ICGtesting.com
Printed in the USA
FSHW011501080321